Thomas Douglas Forsyth

Memorandum on Routes From The Punjab To Eastern

Turkistan

Thomas Douglas Forsyth

Memorandum on Routes From The Punjab To Eastern Turkistan

ISBN/EAN: 9783744791786

Printed in Europe, USA, Canada, Australia, Japan

Cover: Foto ©Andreas Hilbeck / pixelio.de

More available books at **www.hansebooks.com**

MEMORANDUM

ON

Routes from the Punjab to Eastern Turkistan.

By T. D. FORSYTH, Esq. C. B.,

COMMISSIONER AND SUPERINTENDENT, JULLUNDER DIVISION, PUNJAB.

.

MEMORANDUM

ON

Routes from the Punjab to Eastern Turkistan.

THE President of the Royal Geographical Society in his address at the last anniversary meeting of the Society has remarked on the grand and impassable mountain region lying between the Central Asiatic countries occupied by the Russians and our great Empire of India, and the complete separation of India from Eastern Turkistan.

Similar opinions regarding the "impassable bulwork of the Himalayas and the mighty barrier of the Kuen Luen, whose mountains rise like a wall 17,000 feet high, with scarcely a crest or depression throughout the entire extent," have been given forth by writers at different times, but now they have received from the mouth of the learned President the fiat of authority, as he refers for a confirmation of his opinion to an article in the *Edinburgh Review*, which he tells us was written by an efficient public servant in India.

Now if official information is to be quoted as the basis of opinions delivered *ex cathedrâ* by so important a personage as the President of the Royal Geographical Society, it is necessary that such information should be correct.

Whatever may be the opinion of writers at a distance, it is a fact well known to traders and officials on the spot, who have given their attention to the subject, that the Himalayan range, so far from being impassable to traders or even armies, has been already crossed by both, and abounds in easy routes hitherto perhaps but little frequented, owing not to any insurmountable physical difficulties, but to political or fiscal opposition, and now being opened to general traffic.

The most valuable information on the subject of routes to Central Asia hitherto put forth, is that contained in a letter and memorandum submitted by Captain Montgomerie, R. E., on the 20th July 1861, to the Punjab Government, and published in Mr. Davies' Report on Trade.

The whole paper is well worth perusal, but the following extracts are given for convenience sake here :—

" There are several routes from the Punjab to Eastern Turkistan, but three only are ever likely to be available for traffic—the first is *viâ* Kashmir, and Leh; the second *viâ* Mundee, Kullu, and Leh ; the trial *viâ* Simla, Garoo, and Rudok. The Kashmir route is either direct *viâ* Skardo or by Ladak ; the Mundee road starting from Noorpore, Umritsar, or Loodianah goes by Kullu, and the Simla route either *viâ* Sooltanpore, Kullu, and the Baralacha Pass, or by the Parunz La (Pass), or avoids Ladak altogether, traversing the Chinese territory, but all, except the latter, cross the Karakorum Pass."

The most direct route to Yarkund, taking the sea at Kurrachee as the starting point, is that *viâ* Mooltan, Jhelum, Kashmir and Skardo, but as pointed out by Captain Montgomerie, " it is not generally well adapted for traffic."

" The next route *viâ* Jhelum, Kashmir, and Leh to Yarkund is, in Captain Montgomerie's opinion, 'not only the shortest but the best and cheapest route for traffic from the sea to Eastern Turkistan.' From Jhelum to Leh (Ladak), the route through the mountains is better than any other that traverses the Himalayas ; the road between the plains and Leh crosses the Himalayan range by a very remarkable depression of only 11,300 feet, and none of the passes on it exceed 13,300 feet in height, and they are, moreover, open for at least seven or eight months in the year, and could be crossed at any season in fine weather. There is, moreover, between the plains and Leh but one or at the most two halting places without a village in the vicinity, in itself a very great advantage."

The next route in use is that *viá* Mundee and Kullu.

" The greater part of the traffic between the Punjab, Leh, and Turkistan is carried on by this road, and after the road *viá* Kashmir and Leh, it is decidedly the best route from the Punjab to Eastern Turkistan, Yarkund, &c.; though the passes between the Chenab (Chundra Bagha) and the Indus are very high on this route, yet the slopes are so easy that there is but little difficulty in crossing. The route is open for about five or six months, being nearly two months less than the Kashmir route. There are, moreover, nine or ten marches over very elevated bleak mountain land without any villages. To the east of the Baralacha, there is no route well adapted for traffic with Eastern Turkistan."

Captain Montgomerie then gives the following comparative distances by the three routes :—

1st—

		Miles.
To Mooltan by river	...	750
Thence to Jhelum by river	...	350
Jhelum to Kashmir	...	192
Kashmir to Leh	...	256
	TOTAL	... 1,548

2nd—

To Mooltan	...	750
Thence to Lahore	...	300
Lahore to Umritsar	...	35
Umritsar to Sealkote	...	64
Sealkote to Kashmir...	...	195
Kashmir to Leh	...	256
	TOTAL	... 1,600

3rd—

As above to Umritsar	...	1,085
Umritsar to Noorpore	...	90
Noorpore to Mundee	...	112
Mundee to Sooltanpore	...	36
Sooltanpore to Leh	...	287
	TOTAL	... 1,610

Taking Umritsar as the starting point, Captain Montgomerie gives the distance to Leh by the Kashmir route at 40 marches, or 515 miles, and by the Mundee route at 41 marches, or 525 miles, over a very much more difficult country.

But it was then pointed out that, owing to the heavy Customs duties in Kashmir, the Kullu route was most frequented. Captain Montgomerie then remarks that :—

" Every endeavour should be made to improve the roads when a small outlay is likely to be effectual, and if possible camels should be taken as far as Kullu. The Kashmir road offers great facilities for allowing camels to pass, and a very small expenditure would be sufficient to make the present road passable for camels. The double-humped camel has been brought to Leh several times, and it is capable of carrying burdens over the highest passes. Ladakh itself offers but few obstacles to the passage of camels."

According to the state of affairs as represented by Captain Montgomerie, Leh, the capital of Ladak, was the point farthest north to which he carried his comparison of routes, that place being the great market for exchange of goods between Central Asia and Hindoostan. And as is clearly shown by him, the choice lay between the route from Umritsar *via* Kashmir to Leh, and that *via* Mundee-Kullu to Leh, the difference between these two routes being one march or 10 miles in favor of Kashmir in actual distance, besides crossing lower passes, and being open for many more months in the year. Moreover, it was then the case that camels could be taken for 15 marches along the Kashmir route, and only 10 marches along the Kullu route.

But since 1861 great changes have taken place, and it is proposed now to consider the comparative merits of the different routes to Yarkund.

Taking Leh as still the great entrepôt of Central Asian commerce, though it will be shown hereafter that this is likely to be changed, we may view the improvement made on each line.

When Captain Montgomerie wrote, there was no Mooltan and Lahore Railway, and his calculation of distances by water will have to be set aside.

We may take Umritsar as our starting point, that being the chief emporium of trade, and we know that the Maharajah of Kashmir desires all trade to pass by Jummoo, and will give every facility to traders by that line. The road from Jummoo over the Bunuhal Pass to Kashmir is not so easy as that by Jhelum, though the pass to be crossed is lower. In a few years time the railroad to Rawul Pindee will be opened, and possibly this may cause some alteration in the point at which Kashmir is entered. As the Maharajah has lowered his duties, and perhaps ere long may abolish transit dues, it may be taken for granted that in a few years time, fiscal considerations will have no weight in determining the line taken by traders.

It may safely be predicted that there will be a vast increase of trade along this line, and perhaps the greater advantages of the Kashmir route with its frequent villages may induce mer-chants to take that line in preference to another shorter one.

As our object is to extend trade without obtaining any monopoly or preference for any one route, every improvement made or facility offered by the Maharajah will be welcomed as proving the identity of his interests with ours.

We may now review the improvement made or contemplated on the Kullu line.

In the first place, a cart road is under construction through-out the whole length of the Kangra valley. At present it is only to extend to Palumpore, but Wuzeer Goshaon, the energetic Prime Minister of Mundee, is anxious to continue the road to the salt mines at Goomah, and this work, it is hoped, may be completed in a few years.

Goomah is 16 marches from Umritsar.

As the Rawul Pindee railroad has been mentioned, it is only fair to take into consideration the possibility of a railroad to Puthankot, the project for which is already under the consideration of the Government.

From Goomah a new road over the Bubboo Pass has been made to Sooltanpore-Kullu through Mundee territory, thus saving one march of 15 miles. The road was originally intended only for mules, but the gradient is so easy that there will be no difficulty in taking camels over it when it has been properly widened. Once in Kullu camels can travel with perfect ease up the Bias valley as far as Pulchan, the foot of the Rotang Pass, a distance of 23 marches from Umritsar.

From Pulchan to Leh, the road is passable for laden mules, and that portion through Lahoul is being improved with the slender funds placed at the district officer's disposal. Supplies are collected at every stage, and *serais* are being built at the most desolate halting places in British territory.

Thus instead of the Kashmir route being 10 miles shorter as formerly, it is now 5 miles longer, and instead of camels going 15 marches on the Kashmir route, and only 10 on the Kullu road, they will be able to go 23 marches on the latter road, or, still better, carts can be taken for 16 marches to Goomah.

At present the rates of carriage hire are considerably lower by Kashmir than by Kullu, a difference of Rs. 7 or 14 shillings per horse load being in favor of the former road.

This is owing chiefly to the exceptionally high rates charged in Lahoul, arising out of the physical difficulties which formerly existed, but are now being removed.

Formerly no laden animals could cross the Rotang Pass, and merchandize had to be transported on men's backs. When the trader reached Lahoul, he found himself at the mercy of the inhabitants, who fixed their own terms for the hire of cattle, and often subjected the traders to great annoyance. To such a degree did they carry their annoyance that ever since the road has been made passable for animals, they have tried to assert their right to the monopoly of carriage, and in many ways caused inconvenience to merchants.

Arrangements have now been made for increasing the supply of carriage in Lahoul, and traders have been informed that no monopoly of carriage is allowable. But though improvements have been made on this road, there is still much left to be done, if we would see trade flowing throughout the line without any interruption. When the trade shall have acquired sufficient importance, if it be considered not to have attained that point already, it may be hoped that a proper staff of engineers may be appointed with suitable funds to render the small piece of road from the Rotang to the Lingtee, a distance of 10 marches, as feasible for traffic as the Hindoostan and Tibet Road has been made. At the outside, the whole cost could not exceed half a lakh of rupees.

From Lingtee, the boundary of British territory to Leh, the road passes over two easy sloping passes, 17,000 feet high, and crosses a large level plain. The road is perfectly practicable for laden animals, but would be of course improved if labor were applied to it every year.

But we may now consider the effect produced on the different routes by opening out the line between Yarkund and Leh by the Changchenmoo valley, by which the Karakorum Passes are avoided.

Regarding the advantages of this route over all others, we have not only the testimony of Mahamad Amin, guide to Adolphe Schlagentweit, as also of Mr. Johnson, but this year the road has been thoroughly examined and reported on by Dr. Cayley, who has satisfied himself that as far as the head of the Karakash river, there is no obstacle whatever to the passage of camels and laden animals of all descriptions. From the Karakash to Yarkund, no difficulties exist, and at a meeting of traders held in Leh in September last, the traders expressed an unanimous desire to see this route brought into general use. The Yarkund Vakeel, who was at the time in Leh, on his return to his own country, not only expressed his concurrence, but is now on his way to Yarkund by that route.

Why a road so free from difficulties should have remained closed so long, and why merchants should have been compelled to take the distressing and difficult route of the Karakorum has not been satisfactorily explained, but we may hope that in future it will be abandoned. And in any case we have established the fact beyond all controversy that the statement regarding the Kuen Luen range rising like a wall to separate Hindoostan from Turkistan without any depression is quite a fiction.

With the prospect then before us, of seeing this route opened to general traffic, I have just travelled over Ladak to ascertain whether shorter routes to Hindoostan cannot be found than that which passes through Leh.

Starting from Leh, the road to the Changchenmoo proceeds along the bed of the Indus in a south-easterly direction for two marches to Chimira, and then striking northwards across the Changla Pass, 17,040 feet high, takes an easterly direction along the Tanskie valley to the Pangong Lake, six marches from Leh, where it enters soon afterwards to the Changchenmoo valley.

Now a glance at the map will show that traders from Hindoostan coming by the Mundee-Kullu route* would reach the Changchenmoo and Leh route at Marshelling opposite to Chimira. But unless the object of the traders were to go to Leh for the sake of changing carriage or for other purposes, I have ascertained by personal examination that a much shorter and remarkably easy route can be taken from the Pangong Lake to the Lingtee (Lahoul).

* Marked red on the map.

This route† starts along the south bank of the Pangong Lake for 12 or 14 miles, and then passes over broad undulating plains to the Indus, along which it runs for about 15 miles till the village of Modh is reached at the end of the fourth march. A still shorter route to Modh from Chushul over an easy pass is indicated by Mahammed Amin as being passable for ponies.‡

† Marked blue on the accompanying map.

Pangmik to Meyrick	1
Chushul	2
Chagga	3
Modh	4

‡ But if this line were taken, it would pass by Puga, and join the old line at Rukchin.

From Modh the new route would cross the Indus and reach the south of the Chomourire Lake in three marches. Thus far the road from Yarkund is perfectly practicable for camels; grass, fuel, and water are to be found at every stage south of the Changchenmoo, and north of that line we have Dr. Cayley's authority that at only one or at the most two stages are grass and fuel difficult to be procured.

From the south of the Chomourire Lake, the road would proceed westwards to the Pangbok Pass, not yet visited by me, but reported by the inhabitants of Roopshu and by traders who have crossed it to be very easy, and with a little expenditure of money and labor it might be rendered completely passable for all animals.‖

‖ Since writing the above, I have perused Captain, now Major General, Cuningham's report on the boundaries between Ladak and British territory, and find that 21 years ago, he advocated

Across the Pangbok, the road would be taken along the banks of the river Tsrap or Cherap for one march till it joined the Kullu and Leh road at Lingtee. This road from the Chomourire is even now used for traffic at certain seasons of the year.

By this route, two high passes and five marches are saved between Lahoul, the extremity of British territory, and the Changchenmoo, and as merchants desire, as evinced this year at Leh, to trade direct with Yarkund, this route will be found most advantageous and cheap.

At present the cost of hiring a horse to carry goods from Umritsar to Yarkund is Rs. 72 to Rs. 75.*

* This rate, it is hoped, may be reduced when the Changchenmoo route is brought into use.

Now, when camels can travel as far as Pulchan, the foot of the Rotang on the south side, and as far as Kiundong, south of the Chomourire on the north side coming from Yarkund, there will be only 14 marches left for goods to be transported on ponies or yaks, even if the interests of the traders are not sufficiently important to justify

opening out this same route. I give the following extract from his report :—

"As there was a well trodden foot-path up the left bank of the Cherpa (or Tsrap), and as the Lahoules, who were with us, stoutly denied all knowledge of it, it seemed certain that this must be one of the principal routes used by the smugglers of shawl wool between Rudok and Lahoul. As we could obtain no information regarding this route, we determined to despatch a trustworthy party up the Cherpa, who should rejoin us at the Chomourire Lake, as we had little doubt that the route would end on the southern end of the Lake. On their return, the party reported that they had found a bridge five miles above the junction, and that the pathway was perfectly practicable even for laden animals, with the exception of an extensive landslip near the head of the Cherpa river. Several traders' or shepherds' encampments were noticed on this route, where both grass and fuel were procurable in the neighbourhood of the river. They described the pass at the head of the river as being so easy that with a little labour, it might be readily made into a very good one. From thence after a short descent, the route ran over stony alluvial flats along one of the feeders of the Para river, and over a low pass to the southern end of the Chomourire Lake, as we had anticipated. A glance at the map will show that this route leads directly from the shawl countries of Rudok and Gardok via Hanle and the Para and Cherpa rivers to the Lahoul boundary at Phalang danda. Were this route to be opened by the British Government, and a few Dhurmsalas or travellers' houses built at convenient distances, our traders in shawl wool from Noorpore and Rampore would be saved the heavy duties which are now levied by the Maharajah Golab Singh."

the completion of the whole road throughout for camel traffic. The cost of freight may then be calculated as follows :—

Hire of camel to Pulchan, 23 marches	..	..	Rs. 12
„ „ pony and porters to Chomourire, 14 marches		„	14
„ „ camel to Yarkund from „ 30 „		„	12
		Rs. ..	38

i. e., Rs. 38 for 4 maunds, instead of Rs. 72 for 3 maunds as at present.

These rates, however, are conjectural ; the hire of a camel in the plains of Hindoostan is not more than Rs. 8 per mensem for a load of 6 maunds ; whereas here the calculation is at the rate of Rs. 12 to Rs. 16 per mensem for 4 maunds.

It may be at once objected that the idea of camels being found for hire at the Chomourire or in Kullu is quite absurd, and looking at the present state of things, it would be of course out of the question. But all these proposals presuppose the establishment of commercial relations between Hindoostan and Central Asia on a proper footing, when it will be easy to arrange that the caravans from both ends shall meet and exchange their carriage.

At present there is one objection to this line,—that supplies of grain are not to be had. This, however, is an evil easily capable of remedy. More grain is grown in Ladak and Spiti than suffices for the wants of the inhabitants, and this year, owing to the abolition of the oppressive restrictions formerly placed on the export of grain from Ladak, a large quantity has been taken to Rudok in Chinese Tartary. Now Rudok is much farther than the Pangong or Chomourire, and there can be no difficulty whatever in inducing the exporters to take their grain to either of these places, when once they are assured of a good market. A very common objection which arises in mens' minds, and often finds expression in depreciation of the idea that any trade can flourish across these mountains, is derived from the fact that such high passes have to be crossed, such cold encountered, and such hardships endured in marching for many days without coming in sight of villages.

But we are not writing for English merchants, who are accustomed to send their goods by rail, and travel themselves in comfortable carriages. We have to deal with a nation accustomed to all the hardships and fatigue of long caravan journeys. And as everything goes by comparison, let us see what is the state of trade in other parts of Asia.

No one doubts the vitality of the trade between Bokhara and Russia, or between Russia and China. Yet what is the description of the hardships undergone by merchants on these routes ? I quote from Michell's Travels in Central Asia, page 489 :—

" Overcoming in this manner the obstacles which the barbarous Asiatics place in the way of the development of Russian trade, the natural impediments by which nature has cut Russia off from that rich oasis watered by the Syr and Amu remain to be considered. The chief obstruction is presented by a vast extent of barren steppes, traversed however by five principal routes, *viz.*, 1st, from Khiva to Mangyshlak on the Caspian ; 2nd, from Khiva to the western shore of the Sea of Aral towards Orenburg ; 3rd, from Bokhara northwards to Orenburg ; 4th from Tashkend along the eastern border of the Kirghiz Steppe to Troitsk ; 5th, to Petropavlosk ; of these the first named is the shortest, not exceeding 1,000 versts, but it passes through waterless regions infested by pillaging Turkmen, and is for these and other reasons unfrequented. The second route, which is 1,300 versts long, is open to much the same objections, and is therefore equally neglected. The third road, that in ordinary use, leads from Orenburg to Orsk, 225 versts, from thence to Fort No. I on the Syr Daria, 721 versts, offering a safe traversable road for vehicles ; further on, again to the Yang Daria river, about 200 versts, and lastly treads southwards through a completely waterless steppe for 300 versts, from whence to

Bokhara there remains a distance of about 200 versts over sandy but less arid localities. The whole distance from Orenburg to Bokhara is reckoned at 1,700 versts. From the fortress of Orsk to Bokhara, there are forty stages, and as many from Troitsk to Tashkend. Along this last route, good pasture for cattle is found. Still better, however, is the road from Tashkend to Petropovlosk, which is throughout the whole distance passable for wheel carriages, and though it extends across a barren steppe, wells are to be found along it.

" The length of this road is 1,600 versts. It is only lately that certain kinds of goods are transported from Russia into the steppe as far even as the banks of the Syr by means of oxen and carts. The ordinary mode of carrying goods is on camels, which animals are alone capable of supporting the want of water or of drinking water of bad quality, while they can also subsist on the prickly shrubs of the steppes. Goods are despatched by caravans, and only at those seasons of the year when snow hurricanes in winter, and the sultry heat and aridity of summer do not render the steppes impassable. Owing to these circumstances, only two caravans pass between Bokhara and Orenburg during the year, and the number of cattle and men forming the caravan is in proportion to the difficulties to be encountered on the journey. The number of beasts of burden in the caravan is also governed by the supply of water and pasture along the road. The route from Khiva to the Caspian has been abandoned on account of the scarcity of water and pasture. Caravans are from two to two and a half months performing the journey from Orenburg to Bokhara, and *vice versa*. The cost of transporting goods is from five to fifteen roubles, or averaging ten roubles=£1-10 per camel carrying a load of sixteen puds or 576 lbs. avoirdupois. From Orenburg to Bokhara the price paid is 60 copecks per pud, or 5s. 8d. per cwt."

The following description of the extraordinary route by which tea is conveyed to Russia from China is taken from Mr. Lumley's report :—

" A considerable proportion of the tea destined for the Kiachta overland market is sent direct from Hankow down the Yang-tse-Kiang to Shanghaie, some is also sent from Foochow and Canton to Shanghaie ; but most of it is collected in the province of Fukien to the north-east of Canton, from whence it is despatched by land or water to Chuh-Chan. Thence it is conveyed by coolies in the manner described by Fortescue over the mountains to Kin-Chan. Here the tea is loaded in small boats, taking about 200 chests each ; it is then conveyed 40 versts down a stream into the Chen-tang, where it is re-loaded into boats carrying 500 chests. Passing the town of Hankow, the boats emerge into the Eastern Sea, and coasting along reach the river Kisiang, up which they proceed to the town of Shanghaie. Here the tea is re-loaded into larger vessels carrying as much as 1,500 chests, besides other goods. These vessels after leaving Shanghaie proceed along the coast to Tientsin, which place they reach if the weather is favorable in about fifteen days.

" The tea is once more re-loaded at Tientsin into small boats taking about 200 chests, which follow the windings of the stream Barboe, and reach Tienshai, about 22 versts from Pekin, in the space of ten days. From this point, the tea is transported by land on camels and in bullock carts to the frontier fortress Changkea or Kalgan at the great wall, a distance of about 252 versts, and thence across the steppe or desert of Gobi, 1,282, to Kiachta.

" The transport of tea from Fukien to Kiachta occupies two or three months according to circumstances."

From Kiachta the winter route is by Selengisk and Verdne Udinsk, and across Lake Baikal over the ice to Irkutsk, a journey of from seven to eight days.

This winter route is generally available from the middle of January to the middle of April. Lake Baikal is 350 miles long and 40 miles broad ; there is occasionally great difficulty in crossing it in consequence of its surface being free from snow, as it is seldom completely frozen till the snow-fall has ceased.

At Irkutsk, the capital of Eastern Siberia, part of the tea is retained for sale in that province, and of the January arrivals, a portion is forwarded to the fair at Irbit. At this fair, purchases are made for Western Siberia and for the Governments of Prem Kazan, Archangel, Orenburg, Viatka, and Vologda. The tea despatched in February to Tomsk generally remains there during the spring, at which time the roads are impassable, and in the month of May, it is sent from Tomsk to Tiumen, partly by land, but chiefly by water, that is to say by the river Tom into the Ob, from the Ob into the Irkutsk, and thence into the Tara, by which stream it reaches Tiumen about the latter end of June. From Tiumen the tea is conveyed by land to Perm, a journey of about twelve days ; here it is loaded into craft on the Kama, down which river it is carried into the Volga at Kazan, and thence up the Volga to Nijni Novogrod, which place it reaches about the end of July. Nijni is now connected with Moscow by railway, a journey for passengers of twelve hours. The transit from Kiachta to Nijni Novogrod often occupies six months, owing to the delays occasioned by the ice on the rivers, but it is sometimes performed in half the time.

The distances by this route are as follows :—

			Versts.
From Kiachta to Irkutsk	..	..	557
,, Irkutsk to Tomsk	...	..	1,554
,, Tomsk to Tiumen	..	..	1,768
,, Tiumen to Kazan	..	..	1,236
,, Kazan to Moscow	..	..	821
	TOTAL ..		5,936 = 4,452 miles.

The distance from the tea-growing districts to Kiachta is reckoned at 500 versts, making a total of 10,936 versts=7,291 miles, which the caravan tea has to traverse before it reaches the Moscow market.

We are told by Mr. Lumley on the authority of General Kryzanowski that, in consequence of the Tungani insurrection in Chinese (Eastern) Turkistan, and the trade between China and Kashgar being stopped, Central Asia had to go without tea.

Some of the enterprising Tashkend merchants, however, ordered large supplies from the fair at Irbit, a distance of 3,000 versts !

Now from the foregoing extracts, it will be seen that caravans are from two to two and a half months' journey between Bokhara and Orenburg, and cross three large deserts. Between Yarkund and Palumpore, where the fair may be taken to correspond with that at Orenburg, the journey by the route just indicated will take 55 days, and as caravans would only pass during the summer months, when all the snow would have disappeared from the passes traversed, no inconvenience from cold would be felt, and for the rest, there is more water, fodder, and fuel to be found on this route than is to be had on the Bokhara and Orenburg line. It has been said that the road over the Himalayas is only traversable for a short time each year, but so also we find it to be the case on the Russian line, and there is no reason why we should demand impossibilities for our route, or abandon it because we cannot effect what is contrary to custom.

The case as regards tea is still more remarkable. From Kangra to Yarkund is only a journey of two months, just about as long as the tea takes to reach Shanghaic from the Chinese plantations ; from Yarkund to Tashkend the journey takes 20 days, and yet owing to our want of proper intercommunication with Russia, the merchants of Tashkend had to get their tea *via* Irbit, a distance of 5,000 miles, whereas they might have got it direct from Kangra or Hindoostan, a distance of less than 1,000 miles.

A word too may be said on the subject of the great barrier which a mountain, 17,000 feet high, is supposed to offer to trade. Such a remark can only be made by a person wholly unacquainted with the Himalayas. All who have travelled in these regions know that, with the exception of the Rotang, the lowest pass of all, the other passes are approached by long easy inclines over the Rotang; a mule road has been made, and may be still further improved as the increase of traffic shall demand it.

There is no intention in putting forward this paper of endeavouring to create a prepossession in favor of this Himalayan route over the more popular and easy route *viá* Affghanistan. But there is this one present advantage in favor of this mountain line, that no hostile countries have to be crossed. As soon as Kashmir territory is left, the caravans reach Yarkund, the ruler of which country would gladly enter into close relations of friendship with us, and only a few days ago a letter from a tea planter appeared in one of the Indian newspapers, lamenting that, although such excellent prices were to be had for these teas if they could only reach the Russian frontier, this was impossible *viá* Affghanistan, owing to the present unsettled state of affairs and the utter absence of all protection of British interests. Had the Indian tea planter known of this route now pointed out, he might have sent off his teas and realized the high profits, which he says await his grasp.

Briefly to summarise the improvements which have taken place since Mr. Davies' report of 1863 was published. Then the chief obstacles to trade were the heavy duties levied by the Maharajah of Kashmir at Leh and on the frontier of the Punjab, the difficult route over the Karakorum, and the insecurity of the road between Leh and Yarkund; also the rugged and uninviting character of the road between the Punjab and Leh *viá* Mundee and Kullu. Still, with all these difficulties and restrictions, as remarked by Captain Montgomerie, from time immemorial there has always been a trade between Hindoostan and Eastern Turkistan, and the wonder is not that the trade should have diminished, but that it should still survive.

Since then we have seen the following improvements effected. The Customs duties of the Kashmir Government have been reduced to an uniform rate of 5 per cent. *ad valorem*, and all obnoxious cesses and exactions have been abolished. The Maharajah has opened out the route through his territory, and by establishing fairs at Jummoo and Leh has given great inducements to traders to frequent the Ladak market.

It has been satisfactorily shown that an easy, safe, and expeditious route free from obstacles exists, and can be used at once, between Yarkund and Ladak, and if a comparatively trifling expense be incurred, this road can be continued over the Pangbok Pass to British territory, and thus the passage of caravans between Hindoostan and Turkistan will be accomplished with at least as much ease as can be performed by caravans between Bokhara and Orenburg.

Further, we have in our favor the openly announced desire of the ruler and people of Yarkund to trade with us, and their very urgent demand for tea, of which the nearest point of supply is reached much more quickly by the Mundee-Kullu route than by any other. Seeing that the Kangra tea plantations are only 55 days distant from Yarkund, where Rs. 4,=8 shillings per lb., are readily given for inferior kinds of tea ; whereas Calcutta is the next nearest point for China teas to be procured for the Turkistan market, it may be hoped that the Kangra planters will not be slow to avail themselves of the advantages now offered them.

No mention has been made by Mr. Davies or Captain Montgomerie of the route to Yarkund and Kashgar from Peshawur *via* Chitral, which some writers suppose must supersede all other lines. As this route passes through countries infested with fanatical tribes always hostile to, and at present in antagonism with, the British power, it may be time enough for us to discuss the comparative merits of the different routes when they are all equally open. But in addition to the testimony of Mahamad Amin, who describes the Chitral route as the easiest of all, *except* the Changchenmoo, I may mention a fact within my own cognizance. For several days on my journey to Leh, I was accompanied by two merchants, Natives of Boneir, who told me that they had formerly traded by the Chitral route, but last year hearing in Yarkund of the facilities offered to traders by the Ladak route, they came that way. They are now returning by it, and said the superiority of this line was so great that they should always adopt it henceforth.

T. DOUGLAS FORSYTH.

21st September 1868.

REPORT

ON THE

Route to the Karakash River

VIA THE

Changchenmoo Valley and Pass,

BY Dr. H. CAYLEY,

ON SPECIAL DUTY AT LADAKH.

REPORT

ON THE

Route to the Karakash River

VIA THE

Changchenmoo Valley and Pass.

Report on route from Ladakh to Eastern Turkistan *via* Changchenmoo to the Karakash river.

I have the honor to submit the following report on the route to the Karakash river, *via* the Changchenmoo Valley and Pass.

Object proposed to be attained by exploring the route.

1. My object in travelling over this road was to ascertain if it is superior or otherwise, for general purposes of traffic and communication, to the route by Nubra and the Karakorum Pass. I had often heard the Changchenmoo route described as practicable and easy, but at the same time there were conflicting accounts regarding it: sometimes it was said to be unsuitable owing to absence of water and grass, and other objections were made against it. In former years there was undoubtedly a frequented road in that direction, as well as one further east through Chanthang to Khotan, but for many years the Changchenmoo route has been almost disused, and Chanthang is entirely closed by the jealous exclusiveness of the L'hassa Government. The former of these roads was taken by A. Schlagentweit in 1857, and again by Mr. Johnson in his journey to Khotan 3 years ago, but the road which I followed differs somewhat from that taken on either of the above occasions, and is shorter and better supplied with both grass and water.

2. I was accompanied on the journey by Kazi Kutab Dín, the Vakeel of the Maharajah of Kashmir, and I was very glad that he should see and judge of the character of the route, and be able to describe it to his own Government.

Was accompanied by the Kashmir Vakeel, who will be able to report to his own Government on the route.

I cannot help acknowledging the zeal and energy with which he entered upon the undertaking in spite of the most discouraging reports, and the cheerfulness with which he bore the fatigues and discomforts of the journey. The Wazír of Ladákh, Ali Akbar Shah, gave every assistance in our preparations for the journey.

3. In the following itinerary I have not given the exact marches we made either on going or returning, as on the outward journey we were, owing to the ignorance of the guide, more than once led astray from the proper route ; and on the return, from a similar cause, we

Gives the stages, the distances between each. Remarks on state of the route and features of the country. Explains why he did not himself follow precisely this line.

were forced to take double marches as far as Changchenmoo, as at the Karakash river I discovered that our supplies of food had run short. When we left our heavy baggage in Changchenmoo valley, I ordered the servants and coolies to carry on with them provisions for 14 days ; but the guide, an old "shikaree" of great repute in these regions, assured them that by the route he knew we should be back much more quickly, and they without my knowledge only took on enough for 10 days. On this account we had to hurry back at all speed, and met our fresh supplies only after the last morsel of food in camp had been consumed. I have, however, described the exact line of road taken on the return march, but divided the stages into convenient distances, where at the same time water, grass, &c., are procurable at the halting grounds.

4. *Stage* 1*st, Leh to Tikse*—12 miles.—An easy level road first down the Leh valley, then up the right bank of the Indus to the large village of Tikse.

2*nd.   Tikse to Chimre*—16 miles.—Direction south-east up the Indus, and then north-east up the Chimre valley. Road good and nearly level. At Chimre is a large village ; just opposite the entrance of the Chimre valley there is a good bridge on the Indus at Machalang, the 2nd stage out of Leh on the main road from Léh to Lahoul and Kullu.

3*rd.   Chimre to Zingrál,* 10 or 11 miles, north-east up the Chimré valley through the villages of Sakté and Jagar.   The road is good but ascends considerably.   There is no permanent village at Zingral (*Zhing-ral* means the " field decayed or ruined.") There is here an old artificial lake and traces of former habitation and cultivation, but only huts and tents occupied during summer by shepherds.   Grass and fuel are plentiful.   From this place there are two passes over the range of mountains bounding the Indus valley on the north (the Kylás or Gangri range) ; one, the Changlá, goes over to Durgul (Changlá, eastern pass) ; the other, the Kélá, (neck pass) leads direct to Tantsi, and gives half a day's march.   I returned by this pass : it is much higher than the other, being 18,400 feet, and though shorter, the ascent and descent are steep and stony, and it would probably never become much used ; it is now, however, often taken by the traders to and from Rudok to save time.   I would here observe that in the new Trigonometrical Survey Map of Ladákh these two passes, the Kélá and Changlá, are made to lead over from the head of the Ugú valley further to the east, and not from the Chimré valley as is really the case ; this is an error very likely to mislead travellers.   The pass at the head of the Ugú valley, the Ugulá is merely an almost unused foot-track, and leads over into another valley far to the east.

4th. Zingral to Durgu, about 18 miles over the Chang-lá, direction north-east.

The road, which is much frequented leads by a very gradual ascent of about 4 miles to the crest of the pass, which I estimate at about 17,000 feet high. The descent is easy and gradual down a valley which is at first a little stony, but soon becomes wide, smooth and grassy. After about 12 miles, the road turns east over a sandy alluvial spur to the village of Durgu. The pass is excessively easy, and the road does not offer a single difficulty.

5th. Durgu, through Tantsé to Muglib, 15 miles. First south-east to Tantsé 7 miles, where there is a village and Government depot at which stores of all kinds, as flour, barley, ghee, sheep, &c., can be procured; then north-east for 8 miles to Muglib, where there is a small village, and wide grassy camping grounds. The road is good, and nearly level, running along the stream, and generally over smooth lawn-like turf.

6th. Muglib to Lukung, 14 *miles.* First 12 miles south-east along a narrow and almost level sandy ravine to near the head of the Pangong lake; the road then turns north over a plain of deep sand for two miles to the small hamlet of Lukúng (*Lukhúng*—the "fountain god's hollow," or "fountain valley"). The ravine above Muglib evidently once drained the Pangong lake. It widens out in several parts of its course, and contains three or four small fresh water lakes, which are fringed with grass. Along the sandy bed of the ravine, the *Myricaria elegans* and a yellow honey-suckle grow in great luxuriance, and a beautiful yellow-flowered *Clematis* is seen hanging in festoons from the rocks on either hand.

From Lukung a direct road runs south-east along the Pang-gong lake through Chushul to the Indus, and then direct either by Rupshu to Lahoul or by the Parang-lá to Spití. For traders passing between our provinces and Yarkund, this route would save 5 or 6 marches over the one round by Léh, and is everywhere easy. *

7th. *Lukung, through Chagra to Lúnka*, 13 *miles.* The road first runs 7 miles north-east over some gravelly ridges, and up a grassy valley to Chagra, where there is a larger camping and grazing ground of the Pangong shepherds and herdsmen, and which is the last permanent residence in this direction; and then east up a gravelly valley for 6 miles, to a grassy camping ground called Lungka (Lung-kha, "valley snow") at the foot of the Másímik pass. The road is good, and the ascent very easy; wood, grass, and water, are plentiful. The word *Chagra* or *Chaga* means "washing place," and there is a slightly warm spring containing soda which is much resorted to for the purpose of washing new "pattús"—woolen cloth. Small trout abound in the stream. About 2 miles north-east of Lukung, there is a grassy valley, which is every year occupied by traders from Chanthang, who come in the summer with hundreds of sheep laden with wool, salt, &c., which they barter with the Ladakhís and others for grain, flour, cotton goods, and other articles. These men are called Chák-pa (Chagpa—"cut-throats"), and come from Maching, a district about 1 month's journey to the eastward;

---

* NOTE.—The stages on these routes are as follows :—
  1. From Lukung to Man. }   Easy level road along south shore of the Pang-
  2. Man to Chushal.   }   gong lake.
  3 and 4. Chushal over a low pass to the Indus at Chumathang. There are also fords and ferries over the Indus at Myn and Nina, a few miles higher up.
  5. Chumathang to Puga.
     From Puga there are 2 routes, one leading by the Tsomoriri lake and Parangla (pass) reaches Spití in 6 marches. The pass is steep and high, but this route is now often followed by the traders of Spití and Bisahar coming to Léh. The other reaches Rupshu in 2 marches from Puga, and there joins the main road from Kúllu and Lahoul to Ladákh at a point 7 marches distant from Kyelang in Lahoul.

they were formerly a race of Tartar robbers, but have been forced by the L'hassa Government into following the more harmless occupation of trade.

8th.   Lungka, over the Másimik pass to Gunlé, about 18 *miles.* First nearly east for about 5 miles to the top of the pass, which is nearly 19,000 feet high, but its ascent is very easy and gradual. From the crest of the pass the road descends to the north down a narrow valley for about 13 miles to Gunlé, passing through two camping grounds called *Rimdi* (*Ringdí*—the " long valley") and *Pang-long*—(the " grassy valley"). The descent is very gradual, and quite easy for laden horses, and a very little labor employed in clearing away stones, &c., over 2 or 3 miles of the roughest part would make the road quite good. Fuel and grass are found almost everywhere. Gunlé ("winter enclosure") is as its name implies a winter residence resorted to by the Pangong shepherds.

9th.   Gunlé to Gogra, about 20 *miles.* The road first runs north down the Gunlé stream for 7 miles to near Pamchalan on the Changchenmoo river, then turns over a low sandy spur, and runs east up the left bank of the Changchenmoo river for about 7 miles; it then crosses the stream by a ford, and continues north-east over a low mountain ridge, lying in the bend of the river, to Gogra (the " garlic ground") where there is a wide level grassy camping ground covered with bushes of *Myricaria*. Gogra is situated in the upper valley of the Changchenmoo, a few miles above the acute bend that the river takes in the middle part of its course. At Pamchalan, or Pamlan as it is also called, there is quite a jungle of *Myricaria elegans*, and abundance of pasture, and both this place and Gogra are winter pasture grounds of the shepherds. The road is everywhere easy and nearly level, but is rather heavy in places from deep sand and pebbly gravel.

The river at the crossing is about 100 yards wide, and is divided into 3 or 4 channels ; it has a rapid stream, and when at its highest is about 4 feet deep. It runs over a level, shingly, and not rocky, bottom, which very much lessens the difficulty of crossing. The water varies greatly in depth, not only at different seasons, but also at different times of the day. It is always lowest in the morning, begins to rise about noon, reaches its height shortly after nightfall, and sinks again by morning. The daily rise in clear weather is from 12 to 18 inches, and is owing to the melting of the snow of the previous day on the mountain near the head of the river. The river is fullest at the end of May, and again from the middle of July to the middle of August. I crossed it twice on foot, the second time on July 25th, there was then about 3 feet of water in the deepest part. It presented no difficulty of any kind, and would never be any obstacle to traffic like the Shyok river on the other route, as it is, I believe, always easily fordable in the forenoon. Two English travellers who crossed it about a fortnight later than I did, described it as being a little deeper, but their baggage was carried over on yaks without damage.

There is another route, which continues eastward up the left bank of the Changchenmoo river to its bend at Kyám, and which was taken by Mr. Johnson in his journey to Khotan. It is considerably longer than the one I followed, and as the river has to be crossed twice within 2 miles it is no saving in that respect.

10th. From Gogra the road crosses the northern bend of the Changchenmoo river, and runs north-east up the Changlung valley for about 16 miles to near the foot of the pass over the range of mountains bounding the Changchenmoo valley to the north.

The Changchenmoo river from its source first runs east by south to a point a few miles below Gogra and opposite Kyam, it then turns due west, which course it retains to its junction with the Shyok, so that the road crosses it twice. I found this ford less deep than the first, and easier to cross. The water begins to rise about 2 hours earlier than at the first, and attains its height about sunset. The path up the Changlung ("Eastern Valley") was generally very easy over gravelly alluvial slopes, and the ascent very gradual. In a few places the road requires a little making to avoid frequently crossing the stream, which however is not deep. Seven miles above Gogra the Changlung valley widens out into a flat basin, full of hot springs and fountains, and six miles above this it divides into two ravines;—one, with the larger stream coming down from the right or north-east, leads over a high (over 19,000 feet) and rather rough but perfectly easy pass to Nischu, north of the range; we followed this road on the outward journey. The other ravine from the left or north-by-west leads over a much easier pass, at least 1,000 feet lower than the other, and with the most gradual easy ascent and descent. This second pass we discovered on going, and on our return came over it and found the road much the shorter of the two as well as better. At the junction of the two ravines is a lofty pyramidal mountain, scarped at the base, where it displays regular strata of sandstone and slate rocks, dipping from each side towards the centre and meeting at nearly a right angle. This makes a most unmistake-able land-mark. I had cairns of stones erected here and at many other places to mark the road, and in this rainless climate they will last for years.

At the camping ground, and almost everywhere up the valley to within 5 or 6 miles of the pass, fuel and grass were plentiful.

11th. *From the head of the Changlung valley over the pass to Nischu, about 15 miles.* The road at first ascends gradually for about 9 miles in a northerly direction to the top of the pass, then turns nearly east and descends gently along the banks of a small stream for about 6 miles to its junction with another stream from the south-east. The latter leads down from the high pass crossed by Mr. Johnson, and the valley at the junction of the two streams is called in his route maps Nischu ("The two Waters"). This as well as nearly all the names of places beyond Changchenmoo are arbitrary, and quite unknown to the people, even to those who have travelled through the country. The Tibetans have the most fertile imaginations for inventing names, and with the exception of a few well known places they give new names on every fresh occasion that offers.

The route I have just described seems to be by far the shortest and easiest of those over this range of mountains, and the pass much lower than any of the others. There is a pass still further west, which was crossed by A. Schlagintweit, of whose journey I saw frequent traces, but it is much higher and more difficult. It is called *Bao-la* (" Cave Pass") from some caves in the ravine on the south side. This range of mountains is the eastern continuation of the Karakorum range. In the Nischu valley for many miles down there is neither grass nor fuel, and though water is plentiful there is scarcely a trace of vegetation of any kind.

From this point the baggage yaks and other animals were sent back to the other side of the pass, as there was known to be a scarcity of pasture on ahead ; one pony only was taken on by the Vakil, and the baggage was carried by coolies.

I have thus far given the route in short stages, which can be changed at pleasure, as camping-grounds exist almost everywhere, well supplied with grass and fuel, and the marches can be lengthened or shortened to suit the convenience of the traveller.

12*th*. *Nischu to a camping ground on the plain north of the
Changchenmoo range of mountains, about* 22 *miles*. The road
first runs north down the valley for 9 miles, then turns north-
by-west across a series of broad flat gravelly ridges for 5 more
to the edge of a wide level plain, in which the outermost
ridge ends abruptly in a descent of 2 or 3 hundred feet. This
plain (called Zhang-ri-thang—" Mountain Plain") stretches far
away to the north, in which direction it is bounded at a
distance of about 20 miles by a range of rocky mountains
almost bare of snow. Just before reaching the plain, the dry clay
bed of an old lake is crossed. Descending on to the plain, the road
runs nearly due north, making for a castle-like rocky eminence
in the centre of the opposite range, and after about 8 miles meets
with a chain of small fresh water pools and rills lying in a long
shallow hollow or ravine, which forms an excellent camping
ground. The ravine has a direction from west to east, and comes
from the snowy ranges to the south and west. In some seasons
there is here a stream of water, which flows north-east into
Tso-thang lake, 15 miles distant. If there is no water to be
found here on the surface it can I believe always be got by
digging down a few inches, as the ground here never dries
up. Fuel is abundant on the surface of the plain, but there is
no grass; horses however eat the tufts of *Eurotia*, which grow
almost everywhere and constitute the only food of the antelope
in these regions.

13*th*. *From last encampment nearly due north across the
plain to its northern edge, and then down a ravine to a camping
ground near the centre of the opposite range of mountains; total
distance about* 23 *miles*. The road first lies nearly due north
across the plain over sand and gravel for about twelve miles,
then crosses a wide flat-topped gravelly ridge some 3 or 4

hundred feet high and five miles across. This is the actual watershed of the range, and all the valleys to the north run down by more or less tortuous course through a belt of rocky mountains to a second large plain lying fifteen miles to the northeast. From the top of the ridge just mentioned any one of these ravines may be followed, and all contain water and grass in some part of their course. This range of rocky mountains runs in a general direction north-west to south-east, and about its centre rise two remarkable lofty craggy eminences, visible from a great distance as they tower above all the others near them, and between the two over a low pass lies the shortest route, as far as I could judge, though by following the ravine either to the right or left of them, no pass has to be crossed. These two eminences are from one to two miles apart, the more easterly has somewhat the form of a vast dome with a rugged broken surface, the other to the left looks like a square tower with a small central peak or spire rising out of a sloping conical base, conspicuous for the red and purple rocks on its surface. Immediately after leaving the Nischu valley these two peaks form most conspicuous features in the landscape.

After crossing the ridge between the two and turning over a low sandy spur to the right, the road turns north down a gorge through lofty cliffs of white quartz, rising in broken peaks to a height of a thousand feet and upwards, and enters a verdant valley with the mountain slopes green with grass, and a stream of clear water running down the centre, through turfy banks carpeted with flowers. This march may be divided by crossing the large plain in a direction north-by-east to a large lake called Tsothang ("Lake of the Plain"), and encamping on its margin, the water of the lake is somewhat brackish, but quite potable; fuel is found near it, but no grass. On our way out we encamped on the

north side of this lake, but returning we left it six or seven miles
to the east, and thus saved a march.

14th. *From the last camp among the mountains,—twelve
miles north-west, to a place called Thaldat.* The direction is first
north-west over a low pass, then *north* down a wide sandy valley,
and lastly *west* over a wide low gravelly spur to the foot of a
lofty pinnacle-like crag, which terminates one of the spurs of the
central range of mountains and overhangs a second wide plain.
This plain like the first extends far away to the north and east,
and contains several salt lakes, and the surface is over a large
extent covered with white saline efflorescence, in some places a
foot and more in depth ; on the east side of this rock is a verdant
grassy hollow, through which a small stream of clean sweet water
runs north towards the nearest salt lake, though like all the
other streams in this region it sinks into the sandy soil before it
reaches the open plain. Fuel is plentiful all round. Two miles
beyond this and on the west side of the same crag there is a
second path of verdure, surrounding a number of springs and
small ponds of intensely salt bitter water ; one of them is however
only brackish and quite fit for drinking. Both these places were
called Thaldat by the guide, and the name seemed well known
to many of the coolies ; it means " Ice or Snow Ground," and is so
called from a lake of snow about a mile to the north out in the
open plain. It is called *Mapothang* in the new survey map, but
as this word has an objectionable meaning in the Tibetan
language, the name Thaldat given by the coolies, and which
seemed well known, is far preferable.

From this place two roads may be taken ; one leads north-
east across the salt plain to the foot of the mountain on its north
side, and then over the Khatai Diwan (pass) and through a valley
among the mountains to the Karakash. This route, which is des-

cribed by Mr. Johnson in his published report, gives a distance of nearly 50 miles without fresh water and almost without grass; the other route, which I followed, leads north-west along the foot of the mountains to a pass at the west corner of the salt plain, and then traverses a third level plain to the valley at the head of the Karakash. It is shorter than the other, and grass, fuel and water are plentiful about midway.

15th. *From Thaldat, twelve miles north-west along the side of the salt plain, then six miles over a low pass to a valley called by the coolies Patsalung.* The road at first skirts the base of the range of mountains on the south-west side of the salt plain for ten miles, then crosses a wide sandy valley running down from the westward to a small patch of swampy ground at the foot of a rocky spur, where fuel and water are procurable and which forms a good camping ground. The water cannot always be obtained without digging below the surface. From this the road ascends gently up a ravine to the north-west, and crosses a low easy pass six or seven hundred feet high, and descends by an equally gentle slope to Patsalung (the " Soda Valley"), a valley opening out into the south end of a third large plain, which is in great part covered with salt and contains three or four salt lakes. At the lower part of the valley we found abundant fuel and water, and on the sides of the hills leading up to the pass grass was plentiful.

16th. *From the last halting place* 20 *miles nearly due north to a camping ground in a wide grassy valley called Lung-ding, about nine or ten miles from the Karakash river.* The road at first turned north-by-west across a wide sandy valley, and along the base of a range of mountains bounding the third salt plain*

---

* The route taken by A. Schalgintweit in 1857, skirted the N. E. side of this plain, and that followed by Mr. Johnson kept amongst the mountains to the N. E. without emerging on this plain at all.

on its west side, then crossed the plain to its northern corner,
and skirting the east side of a salt lake entered the Lung-ding
(" Valley Plain"), a broad grassy valley containing springs of fresh
water, fuel &c,, in abundance. There is unlimited pasturage for
animals in and around this valley. This march was rather heavy,
owing to having to cross, for ten or twelve miles, a surface of
rough salt, into which the feet sank at every step; much of this
may however be avoided by skirting the sides of the plain and
crossing at the narrowest part about half way, where it is little
over four miles across; by this a few miles are added to the length
of the march. This stage of twenty miles is the longest in the
whole journey without finding water, grass or fuel on the road.

17th. *From the camp in Lung-ding to the Karakash river,*
nine or ten miles.—First north for five miles along the valley,
then north-west by the dry bed of an old lake, and down a
rather steep sandy ravine between banks of boulder alluvium to
the Karakash, some twenty miles from its source.

This river here runs in a gorge 2 or 3 hundred yards across,
and divides into numerous channels, running between beds of
grass and flowers, with granite boulders strewn all about; there
are a few roofless huts on each side of the river, built by
previous travellers.

From this point there is a well-known route down the Karakash river to Shadula, one of the halting places on the road to
Yarkund by the Karakorum pass, and 4 or 5 marches north
of that pass and 8 or 9 from Yarkund. I had with me three men
who had been down the Karakash to Shadula. The distance is
about five marches, and they all described the road as level and
easy, and after the first march abounding in grass, fuel &c.
Lower down the valley contains thick jungle.

It is a much frequented pasture ground of the nomad shepherds of Yarkund and Khotan. Mahomed Amin, who accompanied A. Schlagintweit in 1857, gives the same description of it.

5. In the above route I have given the distance to the valley near the head of the Karakash as *The route detailed gives 16 stages, but merchants could do it in 12 or 13 days.* sixteen marches, but it can easily be reached in twelve or thirteen, and merchants with their laden horses would seldom take longer, as they frequently go 25 and 30 miles a day. On my return journey I reached Leh in 13 marches, walking the whole way, and crossed the pass into the Changchenmoo valley in 5 marches from the Karakash, the baggage being carried all the time by coolies. This route in fact is not longer than that by the Karakorum pass.

6. In discussing the comparative merits of these two routes between Ladakh and Yarkund, I will first *Comparison of the Karakorum route, now generally used, and the Changchenmoo route.* point out some of the difficulties of the Karakorum road that are invariably complained of by the traders and others who have traversed it, and compare them with the worst obstacles to be encountered on the other.

1st. The pass over the Kylas range from Leh to Nubra. *Difficulties of the Karakorum route.* There are two roads from Leh, one leading over the Kardong pass, which is 17,500 feet high, excessively steep and stony, and has nearly 1,000 feet of steep glacier on the north side and cannot be crossed by laden horses. All merchandize coming from Yarkund has consequently to be carried over on yaks at considerable expense, (Rs. 2 is charged for each horse-load), and involving serious delay from the merchandize being often detained from 1 to 5 weeks in Nubra before carriage can be procured. Unladen horses even cross at great risk. The other pass above Leh, the Sabu or Digar pass, though less steep and stony than the Kardong and free from

glacier, is 100 feet higher, is rough and difficult, and laden horses
are seldom taken across; whereas the Changlá over the same
Kylás range on the road to Changchenmoo is lower than the
Kardong pass, has no snow in summer, the ascent and descent are
very gentle and easy, and laden horses cross it without the least
risk or difficulty, and a very little labour would render it perfectly
good for camels. It is by far the easiest pass across this range
of mountains north of the Indus. I have now crossed five of
the passes over this range, and the Changlá was the only one
fit for laden horses.

2nd. The Shyok river, which has to be crossed in Nubra
district, is at some seasons most formidable. The easiest ford is
at Diskit, and when I crossed it in August last year the water
was nearly a mile broad; and as, owing to the force of the
current, this had to be crossed obliquely downwards, it doubled
the actual extent of water. The river was divided into 3 or 4
channels, and was in some places nearly four feet deep, with
a very rapid stream, so that the baggage could only be taken
over on mens' shoulders, and the passage of the river was difficult
and much more formidable than the Changchenmoo could
ever be. The latter is little above 100 yards broad, seldom over
three feet deep, and never unfordable.

3rd. The range of mountains between the Nubra valley
and Upper Shyok takes three days to cross, and opposes two high
passes, both very steep and stony, and on one there is a considerable extent of glacier which is often both dangerous and difficult;
whereas the Masimik pass, between Pangong and Changchenmoo,
though nearly 19,000 feet high, is quite free from snow in summer, and the ascent and descent are very gradual and easy,
and its height is quite lost from being so little raised above the
valley on each side; the next pass leading out of Changchenmoo

to the north is still simpler, and one might ride over both with perfect comfort without once having to dismount. Beyond this there is nothing worthy the name of a pass.

4th. The Shyok river has again to be crossed at Sarsíl (Sasár), and though smaller than in Nubra is deep and rapid, and often difficult. This year already the horse of one of the Hájis with all his property has been carried away in the torrent.

5th. Between Sarsíl and Shadula, 5 or 6 marches, there are two high passes, the Karakorum and the Sukit Diwan, both very rough and stony, and no grass or fuel are found over nearly the whole distance ; on the other route, after the Chang-chenmoo, the only pass is a mere hill of 7 or 8 hundred feet, and nearly the whole way from the Changchenmoo to the Karakash, 6 easy marches, is over smooth level sand and gravel ; water is found at the end of every stage ; fuel grows almost every-where ; and there are only 3 stages without grass, and only 2 of these are successive ; so that in every way this route contrasts most favorably with the Karakorum. None of these roads are very suitable for cattle or sheep, as these animals require so much grass ; but for horses, which eat gram, the Changchenmoo offers no difficulties, as the merchants always carry with them a little barley for fodder.

7. The custom now is to take 2 spare horses for every laden animal, to carry grain and fuel and allow for casualties ; and each year not less than 20 per cent of the horses die on the road from exhaustion and falling among the huge stones that strew the path, from avalanches, and from being lost in the torrents. It is pitiable to see the state in which most of the animals reach the journey's end, and they are seldom able to march again with less than six weeks' or two months' rest. On

Remarks on number of spare baggage horses needed on the Karakorum route, and the casualties among them owing to the difficulties of the journey.

account of these risks and difficulties the hire of a horse to carry
a horse-load (about 200 ℔s) of goods between Leh and Yarkund
is nearly Rs. 50, for little over 30 marches, or at the enormous
rate of nearly 4 annas per ℔. The abovementioned losses are never
likely to occur on the Changchenmoo route, as there are no
difficult mountain passes, no dangerous torrents, no risks of avalanches, and no such rough rocky paths. With very little trouble
and labour expended on the first pass and in the Changchenmoo

The Changchenmoo route might easily be made practicable for camels.

valley (and I am in hopes that the Cashmere
Government will do the little that is required for improving the road), camels might
traverse the whole road with the greatest ease. These animals
in Central Arabia go over much more difficult ground, and the
short-legged variety, which is accustomed to the rugged barren
mountain slopes of the Pamir, is in common use in Yarkund, and
a few years ago a caravan of these animals actually came over the
Karakorum to Ladak ; and I hope therefore that in future years
caravans of camels from Central Asia will be seen wending their
way along the sandy plains of the Tibetan Indus.

8. The Vakeel Kutub Din who went with me is fully alive

Hopes the Cashmere Government will do the little that is required to render the Changchenmoo route easy for travellers.

to the merits of the route, and his reports
will I hope favorably influence His Highness
the Maharaja and gain his assistance in
opening it out to trade. A little labour em-
ployed in a few of the roughest places, a few simple stone huts
erected in the most exposed spots, and a plentiful supply of grain
(such as is now kept at Sarsíl) at the present Government depôt
at Taulse, or still better in Changchenmoo, would remove the few
difficulties the route offers. For many years past this route has

The Yarkund Vakeel who traversed this route reports favorably of it.

been so entirely disused, and merchants and
others have got such wild stories of its difficulties and dangers, mostly of a highly

absurd nature, that they may not readily take to it. The Yarkund Vakeel, Mahomed Nazar, has just returned by it, and has
written back from the Karakash to say that he found it very easy
and reached the Karakash with great comfort, and others will
in all probability follow. I have heard too that there was a more
plentiful supply of water when the Vakil went than when I
traversed the road in July. My sole object in opening the road
is to afford a means of communication between Ladak and the
countries to the north by a way less difficult and dangerous
than the Karakorum, so that the immense expense of carriage
may be diminished, and thus one of the great obstacles to trade
through these regions removed.

9   In my hurried journey, which only occupied a month, for
I was anxious not to be absent a day longer
than necessary, in order that I might meet
the Yarkundi merchants on their first arri-
val at Leh, it was impossible to do more than

The hurried nature of his journey permitted very superficial observations only on the physical features of the country.

make very superficial observations on the physical features of the
country passed through ; but the following slight sketch of
certain points may be of interest.

The Kylas range, which is crossed immediately after leaving
the Indus valley, is almost entirely com-
posed of brittle granite, everywhere break-
ing up into a coarse sandy and shingly

Geological formation of the Kylas range.

debris under the influence of the atmosphere, moisture &c. In
the beginning of July there was no snow on the south side, even
up to a height of 19,000 feet, except in patches and in sheltered
situations ; on the north side the snow fields were lower, but
the continuous snow line was hardly below 19,000 feet.

After passing Tantse the road lies in a narrow valley, between two masses of lofty mountains, that on the south-east being chiefly composed of dark grey granite, and that on the north of schistose rocks, veined in all directions with a tracing of white quartz, and nearer the Pangong lake changing to limestone and gneiss, and conspicuous for the alternate strata of black and white rocks which crop out almost everywhere on the lofty precipitous sides. This valley, a ravine, is hemmed in by lofty cliffs, which are often composed of very white gneiss, and must formerly have been the bed of a river draining the great Pangong lake, the water of which is now about 150 feet below the pass over which it once flowed. Just above Tantse and perched on a narrow ledge of rock is a small gunpa or monastery, the last met with in Ladak in this direction.

Geological formation of the country immediately after passing the Tantse stage.

The shores of the Pangong lake everywhere show traces of the water having once reached high up the mountain sides, and in many places old beaches are very distinct. The water is now extremely salt and bitter, but it was once probably fresh as there are in many places along its shores regular strata of shells 15 or 20 feet above the present surface. I found 3 kinds of shell, a *Lymnœa*, a *Planorbis*, and a small Bivalve the *Cyclas*. These shells exist in myriads, and the two first are similar to the fresh water shells now found in warmer parts of Ladakh. I observed also regular beds of vegetable matter in strata several feet thick, and consisting entirely of long leaves of a water plant similar to one now growing in fresh water streams in the neighbourhood. The only existing animal I could find on the lake was a small shrimp-like crustacean of a reddish color. The people of the neighbourhood say that the water of the lake is

Description of the Pangong lake.

sinking year by year, and have legends of the district having once been very fertile and thickly populated; now it is little more than a sandy desert, and three or four miserable huts at Lukung contain all the permanent inhabitants.

The chain of mountains between Pangong and Changchenmoo is lofty, ranging from 19 to 21 thousand feet, but the sides are everywhere sloping, and the ridges wide and round-topped.

Physical aspect of the chain of mountains between Pangong and Changchenmoo

They consist almost entirely of granite and other igneous rocks. The snow line even on the north side is not much below 20,000 feet, except in sheltered aspects. There was no snow on the pass (19,000 feet) even early in July, though in sheltered places large fields of snow extended much lower down. Vegetation is scanty, but the valleys generally have grass in abundance ; and a *Eurotia*, with dry woody roots, which serve admirably for fuel, is found almost everywhere. I was rather early in the season for flowers, but many *Primulæ, Artemisiæ, Saxifrages,* and other plants common in Ladakh, were just appearing ; and near Gunlé I saw a large patch of a dwarf species of *Eliagnus* at a height of over 17,000 feet.

The Changchenmoo valley is in its upper course wide and verdant, and is a regular winter residence of Pangong shepherds and herdsmen. The

Description of the Changchenmoo valley.

valley though 17,000 feet high is sheltered, and contains unlimited wood for fuel. Gunlé, Pamchalán and Gogra are all winter camps. At Pamchalán and Gogra are regular jungles of *Myricaria elegans*, the bushes growing eight and 10 feet high, with branches spreading wide enough to afford shelter from the sun's rays.

The hot springs up the Changlung valley deserve a few words of notice. Seven miles above its junction with the Changchenmoo this valley

Hot springs of the Changlung valley.

widens out into a small basin about ¼ mile broad and one mile long, full of hot springs and fountains, and the surface of the ground covered with white saline matter, chiefly I believe borax, and other soda salts, including common salt, but I have not yet been able to make a proper analysis. The fountains of hot water are most singular. In one place a boss of stalactite resembling an animal's head, projects out from the side of an overhanging rock, and from its mouth or centre a stream of hot water the size of one's arm shoots out into the river below, with such force that I was unable to hold a thermometer close to the mouth of this natural pipe. In another place a mass of stalactite seven or eight feet high, stood in the middle of the river, and from its summit two jets of hot water shot upwards like artificial fountains. The temperature of the first spring was 120° when the stream below was 45° F. All about the flat valley were small pools of warm water, fringed with luxuriant grass of a deep green colour, and along the sides of the stream and among these pools innumerable minute jets of hot water rose up the height of a few inches. Rocks of quartz, stalactite, and variegated coloured clays and clay slates, assuming most fantastic forms, were scattered about among the springs, and occasional patches of snow occurred within a few feet of the hot water. I noticed Brahminee ducks (" *Casarca Rutila*"), a diver and a species of snipe amongst the hot springs. There are also hot springs at Kyám, where the Changchenmoo river bends round to the west.

The mountains north of Changchenmoo are the eastern con-

Physical appearance of the mountains north of Changchenmoo.

tinuation of the Kárákorum range. The main ridge is lofty, and nearly all the passes are over 19,000 feet high, and the peaks 1,000 to 1,500 feet higher, but the mountains are generally rounded with sloping sides, so that the passes are very easy to cross. In July the snow on the northern face was lying pretty generally as low as 18,000 feet, and in the sheltered aspects much lower.

The lowest pass, by which we returned, was quite free from snow. The spurs running south from this range are at the lower parts chiefly composed of unstratified clays of various colours, red, purple and yellow, mixed with stratified slate rocks; higher up the rocks are chiefly slates and sand-stone, and the top of the ridge is granite. On the north side of the range the mountains presented a very different appearance, being everywhere broad and rounded, and rocks *in situ* scarcely anywhere visible, having, as it were, melted away under atmospheric influences, and crumbled into heaps of sand slaty shingle. Even the tops of the highest peaks and ridges are covered with this debris of the rocks beneath, there being no water force to wash it away. Here and there cliffs and pinnacles of sand-stone or lime-stone project through this gravelly covering. The valleys are broad and shallow, filled up apparently by the same debris, which is brought down by the slowly melting snow, and are nowhere cut into deep channels and ravines as is generally the case in Ladakh.

North of this range is the first of the vast lake plains traversed in the route to the Karákásh. It is about 20 miles across, north and south, and much wider in the direction east and west. It is bounded to the west by a lofty range of rugged mountains with snow-clad peaks at a distance of of 20 miles. The region to the west of this range is totally unexplored, and no native seems ever to have visited it; but I have little doubt that by a careful examination a much easier way could be discovered to Yarkund than that by the Karakash.

Description of the 1st lake plains lying north of the eastern continuation of the Karakorum range of mountains.

The mountains present deep gaps between the high peaks, so that there must be low easy passes, and once across the range one comes into the water-shed of the Yarkund river, along the course of which there is in all probability an easy route to Yarkund, or at least to the point where that river crosses the Karakorum route, north of the pass of that name. Should such a route be found it would save the discomfort and trouble of crossing the salt plains, and most likely prove the shortest and easiest way.

To the eastward the mountains are more distant, and generally appear lower, though they present some very high snowy peaks. The surface of the plain is generally a coarse sandy clay and gravel often covered with salsolaceous plants, chiefly a tufty *Eurotia*, with thick woody roots, which, even when quite fresh, burn very briskly, and are the only fuel procurable. This plant quite replaces the Tibetan furze call'd " *Dama* " a species of *Caragana*, which is found under similar conditions in Rupshú—Spiti, &c., but seldom occurs north of the Indus. Were it not for this plant these regions would be almost impassable for want of fuel. It is called in Tibetan " *Gapshen*, " and there are two varieties of the plant, which is found in almost all situations, on the dry sandy plains and on the barren mountain slopes, between the Indus and the Karákásh rivers.

Another plant of the Umbelliferous order, an *Aster*, called by the natives " *Palu*," and which is used by the Lamas for incense, is also found in many places in these regions. It too grows in spreading tufts, and has dry woody roots, which burn well, but the roots are too thin to be of much use for fuel.

Flora of this tract.

A considerable extent of the surface of this plain is composed of a bed of fine lacustrine clay, sometimes rising in low cliffs and ridges, containing

Geological formation.

regular strata of dry water-weeds, resembling those at Pangong lake. I could find, however, no traces of shells or fossils. In this plain I saw two large lakes, one close to the northern edge, called Tso-thang—before mentioned; the other a few miles further south. There are also said to be some larger lakes to the eastward. The level of the plain is about 17,000 feet above the sea. Antelopes are seen in great abundance on the plain, and a few kyang (wild horse); they feed on the young shoots of the *Eurotia*.

The ranges of mountain north of this plain are in great part composed of slate rocks, but the lofty craggy ridges in the centre are chiefly of lime-stone, sand-stone and quartz. The spurs running down to the northwards are generally of clay slate of variegated colours, arranged in thin brittle flakes, and the strata much contorted. The saline springs and efflorescence seem to be almost always connected with this particular formation. In this range are numerous antelope, kyang, and wild yák. I also observed traces of wolves. The only birds I saw were a few ravens and mountain finches, but I found the remains of a deserted eagle's nest, which contained many hundred antelopes' horns, several horses' shoes, and other strange articles.

General aspect of the mountain range north of the 1st lake plain.

The second plain north-east of this range is about 16,000 feet above the sea. It stretches far away to the north-east and east, but is broken up by low ranges of hills. It contains numerous salt lakes, and the surface is over a considerable extent deeply covered with saline matter.

Altitude of the 2nd lake plain.

About a mile from the halting place called Thaldat is one of these lakes, the northern part of which is all salt water; but the southern half forms a lake of frozen snow lying out in the open

Lake at Thaldat consists in northern part of salt water, while the southern half is frozen snow.

plain, and nearly two miles from the nearest hills, which themselves were quite bare of snow on the 15th July.

This snow lake was about 2 miles long, $1\frac{1}{2}$ broad, and 8 or 10 feet deep, with a few inches of clear water running below the snow. On crossing it I could see in the fissures and crevices, that, a foot or two below the surface, the snow was frozen into semi-transparent green ice exactly resembling glacier ice. It is in fact a glacier out in an open plain and not fed by snow mountains. I imagine that in winter an immense drift of snow is heaped up against the hills to the south by driving north winds, and that this lake or hollow is filled with such an accumulation that it does not melt in the short summer of these regions. Northwest of this plain, and separated from it by a range of mountains which we crossed by a low pass, is a third plain of a similar character, also containing several salt lakes. The northern half is covered to a depth of several feet with saline matter, soft, white and powdery on the surface but hard and crystalline below. The surface is often rough like the waves of the sea, rising up in ridges of solid salt 6 and 8 feet high, and sinking into hollows of the same depth. With the afternoon winds this salt was blown up in driving clouds, like dust-storms in the plains of India, which combined with the hot sun and cold dry air were most irritating to the skin and eyes. The glare from the surface also was very trying, and produced effects like snow-blindness. I observed the Tartar coolies make what to me was a novel use of their pigtails. They unplaited them and tied them across their eyes to protect them from the glare. This plain continues uninterruptedly to the valley at the head of the Karakash, without any intervening

Description of the snow lakes.

3rd lake plain similar to the others.

Remarks on unusual saline efflorescence on this plain drifting about in high wind like dust, and the glare producing effects like snow blindness.

mountain range, though in the latest survey map* a ridge is made
4th lake plain described. to cross it nearly in the middle. West of this
plain, but separated from it by a rugged mountain ridge, is a fourth
plain of like nature and containing a large salt lake. Into this
we were conducted by the mistake of the guide, who promised a
short cut across the mountain. On reaching the fourth plain we
discovered our error, and had to return over the intervening range,
and at nightfall found ourselves on the side of the rough field of
salt already mentioned, and had to encamp without fuel or water,
and consequently without food ; the next morning had a march of
10 miles over the salt before we reached water. The thermometer
in the morning stood at 4° F. or 28° below freezing point. At its
northern extremity the third plain ends in the Lungding valley,
which after 4 or 5 miles suddenly dips down by a narrow sandy
ravine to the Karakash river, which is here about 15,500 feet
The Karakash river, and its source and altitude. high. Its source is in some glaciers and snow
fields among high granite peaks to the north-
east. These plains have all evidently once been vast lakes, probably of fresh water, and draining into the Karakash river. On
the sides of the surrounding hills up to a height of 150 feet are
seen old beaches rising in regular terraces. The mountains round
are chiefly slaty, with peaks of granite and other igneous rocks.

The mountains north of the Karakash are granite, exactly
Appearance of mountains north of the Karakash river. resembling the brittle granite of Ladák.
South of the river slate rocks prevail. Over

---

* The arrangement of these mountains in this map is incorrect. The dark ridge marked
as running nearly east and west in latitude 35° 33' and 34' and east longitude 79° 20' to 30'
does not exist in this direction. This ridge in reality runs nearly due north, and separates
the " salt lake" south of the " encampment Karakash " (of map) from the larger " salt lake" to
the south west ; and in the situation that this range is made to occupy in the map there is what
I have described as the third salt plain, an immense level expanse, 20 miles long north and south
and from 5 to 15 or 16 miles across in the opposite direction, and containing 4 or 5 salt lakes.
It is separated by the range I have just noticed as lying nearly north and south from the fourth
salt plain.

all these regions antelope are common, and near the Karakash I saw kyang, and traces of wild yák (Droug) also a few hares, brahmini ducks, and a species of snipe.

Over the salt plains there is little or no vegetation, except the *Eurotia*, and even this does not grow where there is much salt; but amongst the mountains between the two first plains some

Salt plains have little or no vegetation. Flora of mountains between these plains.

Artemisiæ and the *Eurotia* were plentiful; here too the slopes were clothed with grass, *(Carex)*, and many flowers, chiefly *Primulæ*, a *Ranunculus* and *Saxifrage*, and a very handsome yellow *Ligularia* grew along the sides of the springs. At the head of the Karakash the ground was carpeted with bright flowers. A yellow *Primula*, the *Androsace*, grew in wide patches. Two or three species of *Saussu ea*, some small *Cruciferæ*, a blue *Nepeta*, a liguminous plant not in flower, *Saxifrages*, and several other plants besides the *Eurotia* were common, but there were no shrubs or vegetation of larger growth.

10. With regard to climate, the most striking points are the extreme dryness, and the extremes of heat and cold. In Changchenmoo valley on

Remarks on climate of the route traversed.

July 9th at a height of 17,000 feet above the sea, the thermometer was 31° at sunrise, 75° at noon in a tent, and 212° (a black bulb sun thermometer) in the sun's rays. On the 25th July in the same place it only sunk to 40° at sun-rise.

On the first plain, on July 13th and 14th the thermometer at sunrise was 10° and 13.° July 22nd on the same plain it was 19° at sunrise.

Temperature of first salt plain.

On the third salt plain (elevation 16,000 feet) the thermometer on July 18th stood at 4° at sunrise.

Temperature and elevation of the third plain.

At Lungding near the Karakash on July 19th and 20th, the minimum temperature was 22° and 24°. It was evident that extreme nocturnal cold lasts the greater part of the year on these elevated plateaus, and it probably freezes every night. The cold was, however, decidedly less towards the end than at the beginning of July. On the evening of July 16th it began to snow, and continued nearly all night, and in the morning the whole plain was covered to the depth of an inch or two ; this all disappeared in a few hours. Rain is probably unknown in these regions.

In the valley of the Karakash we seemed suddenly to enter

Climate of the valley of the Karakash.

a warmer climate, so great was the contrast after the open plains, and the more advanced state of the vegetation showed the same. In the day-time the heat of the sun was intense. I was forced to leave my sun thermometer in Changchenmoo, but I am sure that the sun was as hot on the northern plains as in that valley, where the thermometer rose to 212° (more than 30° above the boiling point of water). There can hardly be another country in the world where the thermometer rises from 4° to 212° in a few hours. The cold at night evidently accounts for vegetation being so scanty, even in places well supplied with water. All the lakes, fresh and salt, and generally the running streams, were partially frozen in the mornings.

Another point to be noticed in the climate was the constancy

Prevailing winds.

and the regularity of the winds.

During the forenoon the wind was always light and uncertain, blowing more or less from the south. In the afternoon it veered round to the west and north-west and blew steadily, and by evening rose to almost a hurricane from the same quarter ; three or four hours after sunset it fell again, and went round to the north, and in the morning blew a gentle but cold air from the east. This occurred every day, but the further north we went the earlier in the afternoon the westerly wind rose and the greater was its violence.

I did not observe the almost cloudless skies of Ladák proper, but noticed that clouds blew up almost every afternoon and disappeared again during the night. This may have been accidental, as there has been more than the average of cloud this season in Ladák itself.

H. CAYLEY,
On Special Duty.

L A D A K,
18*th August* 1868.

www.ingramcontent.com/pod-product-compliance
Lightning Source LLC
Chambersburg PA
CBHW031801090426
42739CB00008B/1115